MW00785273

C O N T E N T S

IT'S ONLY A PAPER MOON

Words by
BILLY ROSE and E.Y HARBURG

Music by
HAROLD ARLEN

SUGGESTED REGISTRATIONS

	Pre-Set		Spinet		All Electronic Organs
(A♯)	62-8768-000	(U)	82-8768-000	(U)	Full Solo Combination Strings 16', 8', 4', Reeds 8'
[A♯]	00-4544-220	[L]	2544-2200	[L]	Diap. Gamba 8', Flute 4'

Pedal: 5-3	Pedal: 3	Pedal: Bourdon 16', 8'
Vibrato: 3	Vibrato: Normal	Vibrato: Medium

FOR YOU

Words by
AL DUBIN

Music by
JOE BURKE

SUGGESTED REGISTRATIONS

	Pre-Set		Spinet		All Electronic Organs
A♯	52-6070-542	U	72-8070-542	U	Strings 8′, Flutes 16′, 8′, 4′
A♯	00-4544-220	L	2544-2200	L	Diap., Gamba 8′, Flute 4′
Pedal: 4-3		Pedal: 3		Pedal: 16′, 8′	
Vibrato: 3		Vibrato: Normal		Vibrato: Full	

5

THE VERY THOUGHT OF YOU

Words and Music by
RAY NOBLE

SUGGESTED REGISTRATIONS

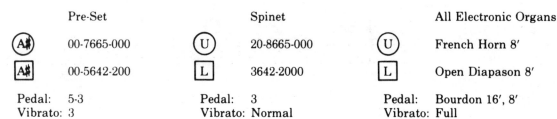

	Pre-Set		Spinet		All Electronic Organs
(A#)	00-7665-000	(U)	20-8665-000	(U)	French Horn 8'
(A#)	00-5642-200	(L)	3642-2000	(L)	Open Diapason 8'
Pedal:	5-3	Pedal:	3	Pedal:	Bourdon 16', 8'
Vibrato:	3	Vibrato:	Normal	Vibrato:	Full

NIGHT AND DAY

Words and Music by
COLE PORTER

SUGGESTED REGISTRATIONS

	Spinet			All Electronic Organs
(A♯) 50-8746-224	(U) 70-8746-224	(U)	Flutes 8′, 4′
[A♯] 00-4544-220	[L] 2524-2200	[L]	Diap., Gamba 8′, Flute 4′
Pedal: 5-3	Pedal: 3	Pedal:	16′, 8′, Medium
Vibrato: 3	Vibrato: Normal	Vibrato:	Full

10

ALL MY LOVE

Words and Music by
AL JOLSON,
SAUL CHAPLIN and HARRY AKST

SUGGESTED REGISTRATIONS

Pre-Set	Spinet	All Electronic Organs
(A#) 20-4625-000	U 40-6625-000	U Strings 8', Clarinet 8'
[A#] 00-4423-220	L 2423-2200	L Flute 4', Strings 4'
Pedal: 4-2	Pedal: 2	Pedal: Flute 8'
Vibrato: 3	Vibrato: Normal	Vibrato: Full

LOVER, COME BACK TO ME!

Words by
OSCAR HAMMERSTEIN II

SUGGESTED REGISTRATIONS

Music by
SIGMUND ROMBERG

YOU'RE MY EVERYTHING

Words by
MORT DIXON

Music by
HARRY WARREN

SUGGESTED REGISTRATIONS

Pre-Set		Spinet		All Electronic Organs	
A#	40-8757-234	U	60-8757-234	U	Full Solo Combination (Strings and Reeds) with 16'
A#	00-6644-322	L	4644-3220	L	Great (No Reeds) 8'
Pedal: 5-3		Pedal: 3		Pedal: Bourdon 16', 8'	
Vibrato: 3		Vibrato: Normal		Vibrato: Medium	

AS TIME GOES BY

Words and Music by
HERMAN HUPFELD

SUGGESTED REGISTRATIONS

Pre-Set		Spinet		All Electronic Organs
A# 52-6070-542		U 72-8070-542		U Strings 8', Flutes 16', 8', 4'
A# 00-4544-220		L 2544-2200		L Diap., Gamba 8', Flute 4'
Pedal: 4-3		Pedal: 3		Pedal: 16', 8'
Vibrato: 3		Vibrato: Normal		Vibrato: Full

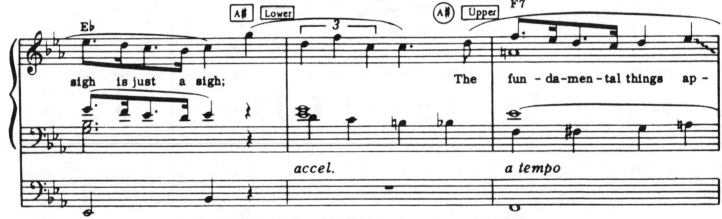

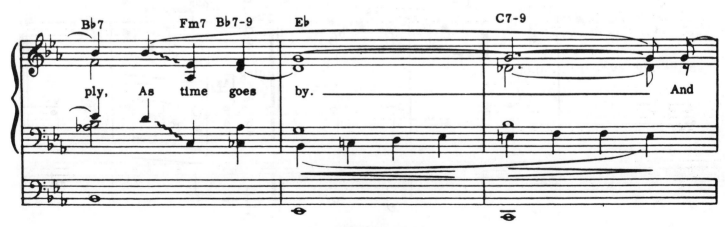

19

TEA FOR TWO

Words by
IRVING CAESAR

Music by
VINCENT YOUMANS

22

I COVER THE WATERFRONT

Words by
EDWARD HEYMAN

Music by
JOHN GREEN

SUGGESTED REGISTRATIONS

Pre-Set		Spinet		All Electronic Organs	
Ⓐ♯	00-8476-000	Ⓤ	20-8476-000	Ⓤ	Flutes 8', 4', Clarinet 8'
A♯	00-5432-200	L	3432-2000	L	Melodia (Fr. Horn) 8'
Pedal: 4-3		Pedal: 3		Pedal: 16', Medium	
Vibrato: 3		Vibrato: Normal		Vibrato: Full	

SECRET LOVE

Words by
PAUL FRANCIS WEBSTER

Music by
SAMMY FAIN

SUGGESTED REGISTRATIONS

Pre-Set	Spinet	All Electronic Organs
(A♯) 52-6070-542	(U) 72-8070-542	(U) ~~Special Strings +~~ Strings 8′, Flutes 16′, 8′, 4′
[A♯] 00-4544-220	[L] 2544-2200	[L] Diap., Gamba 8′, Flute 4′ ~~8′, 2′~~
Pedal: 4-3	Pedal: 3	Pedal: 16′, 8′
Vibrato: 3	Vibrato: Normal	Vibrato: Full

© 1953 WARNER BROS. INC. (Renewed)
All Rights Reserved

27

EMBRACEABLE YOU

Music and Lyrics by
GEORGE GERSHWIN and IRA GERSHWIN

SUGGESTED REGISTRATIONS

Pre-Set		Spinet		All Electronic Organs	
(A♯)	70-8706-000	(U)	70-8706-000	(U)	Flutes 16', 8', 4', 2'
[A♯]	00-5443-211	[L]	3443-2110	[L]	Viola (Str.) 8'
Pedal: 5-3		Pedal: 3		Pedal: Bourdon 16', 8'	
Vibrato: 3		Vibrato: Normal		Vibrato: Full	

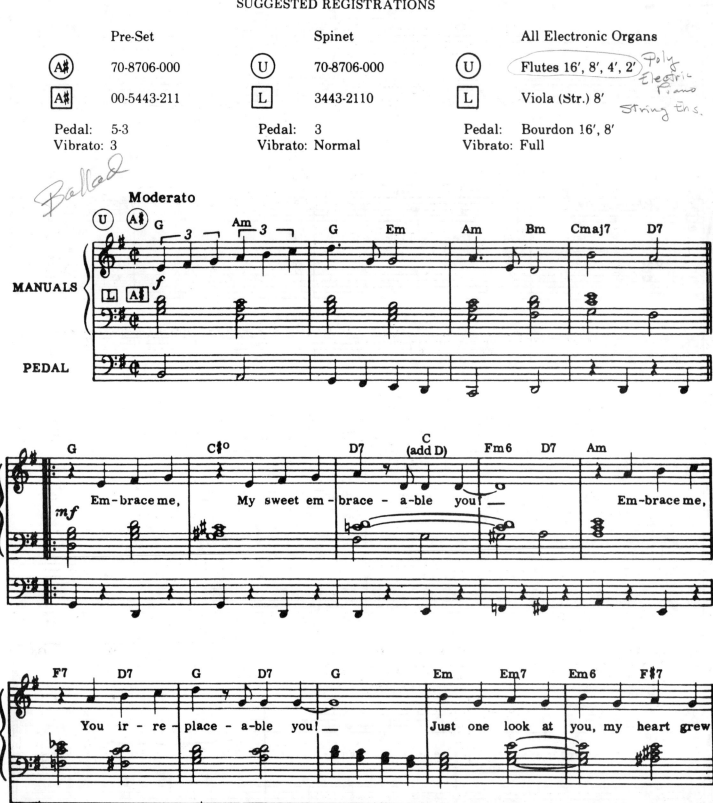

29

EVERGREEN
(Love Theme From "A STAR IS BORN")

Words by
PAUL WILLIAMS

Music by
BARBRA STREISAND

SUGGESTED REGISTRATIONS

Pre-Set		Spinet		All Electronic Organs	
Ⓐ♯	30-5803-000	Ⓤ	50-7803-000	Ⓤ	Flutes 8', 4', Oboe 8'
A♯	00-4423-000	Ⓛ	2423-0000	Ⓛ	String Diapason 8'
Pedal: 4-2		Pedal: 2		Pedal: 16', 8', Medium	
Vibrato: 3		Vibrato: Normal		Vibrato: Full	

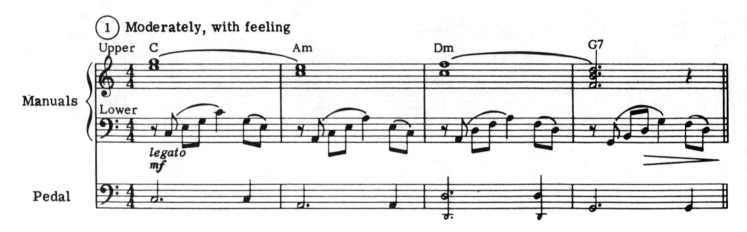

36

GET HAPPY

SUGGESTED REGISTRATIONS

Words and Music by
HAROLD ARLEN and TED KOEHLER

Pre-Set		Spinet		All Electronic Organs	
Ⓐ♯	52-6070-542	Ⓤ	72-8070-542	Ⓤ	Strings 8′, Flutes 16′, 8′, 4′
[A♯]	00-4544-220	[L]	2544-2200	[L]	Diap., Gamba 8′, Flute 4′
Pedal: 4-3		**Pedal:** 3		**Pedal:** 16′, 8′	
Vibrato: 3		**Vibrato:** Normal		**Vibrato:** Full	

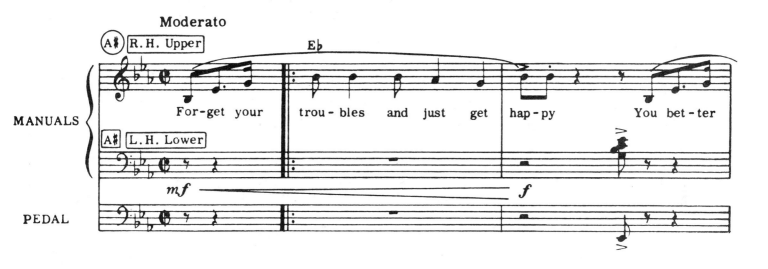

SHADOW WALTZ

Words by
AL DUBIN

Music by
HARRY WARREN

SUGGESTED REGISTRATIONS

Pre-Set		Spinet		All Electronic Organs	
A♯	50-6824-464	U	70-8824-464	U	Flutes 16′, 4′
A♯	00-4544-220	L	2544-2200	L	Diap., Gamba 8′, Flute 4′
Pedal: 5-3		Pedal: 3		Pedal: 16′, 8′	
Vibrato: 3		Vibrato: Normal		Vibrato: Full	

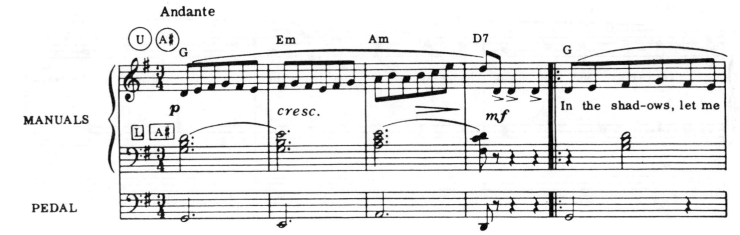

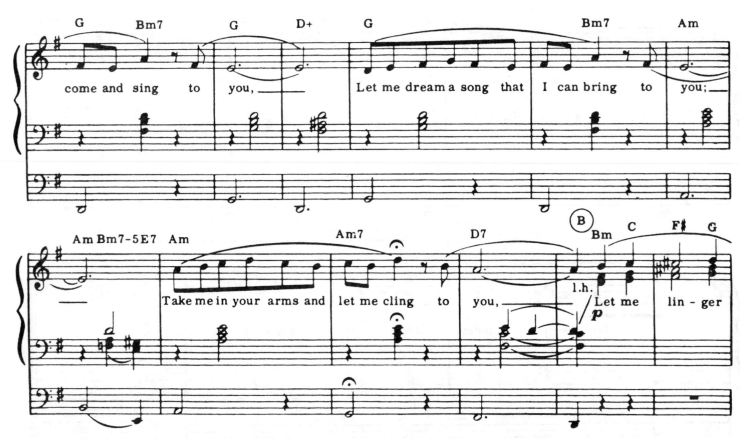

I WANT TO BE HAPPY

Words by
IRVING CAESAR

Music by
VINCENT YOUMANS

SUGGESTED REGISTRATIONS

Pre-Set	Spinet	All Electronic Organs
(A#) 52-6070-542	(U) 72-8070-542	(U) Strings 8', Flutes 16', 8', 4'
[A#] 00-4544-220	[L] 2544-2200	[L] Diap., Gamba 8', Flute 4'
Pedal: 4-3 Vibrato: 3	Pedal: 3 Vibrato: Normal	Pedal: 16', 8' Vibrato: Full

Medium Bright

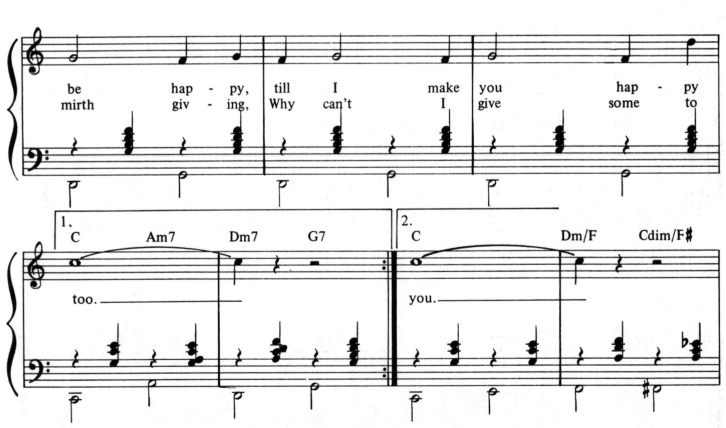

BEGIN THE BEGUINE

Words and Music by
COLE PORTER

SUGGESTED REGISTRATIONS

Pre-Set		Spinet		All Electronic Organs	
(A#)	40-6344-500	(U)	60-8344-500	(U)	Strings 8' and Reeds 8', 4'
[A#]	00-4544-220	[L]	2544-2200	[L]	Diap. Gamba 8', Flute 4'
Pedal: 5-3		Pedal: 3		Pedal: Bourden 16', 8'	
Vibrato: 3		Vibrato: Normal		Vibrato: Full	

MISTY

Words by
JOHNNY BURKE

Music by
ERROLL GARNER

SUGGESTED REGISTRATIONS

Pre-Set	Spinet	All Electronic Organs
(A#) 30-5803-000	(U) 50-7803-000	(U) Flutes 8', 4', Oboe 8'
[A#] 00-4423-000	[L] 2423-0000	[L] String Diapason 8'
Pedal: 4-2	Pedal: 2	Pedal: 16', 8', Medium
Vibrato: 3	Vibrato: Normal	Vibrato: Full

Slowly

Look at me, I'm as help-less as a kit-ten up a
way and a thou-sand vi-o-lins be-gin to
own would I wan-der thru this won-der-land a-

tree and I feel like I'm cling-ing to a cloud. I can't un-der-stand, I get
play, or it might be the sound of your hel- lo that mu- sic I hear, I get
lone, nev-er know-ing my right foot from my left, my hat from my glove? I'm too

mist- y just hold - ing your hand.
mist- y the mo- ment you're
mist- y and too much in

Walk my

TIME AFTER TIME

Words by
SAMMY CAHN

Music by
JULE STYNE

SUGGESTED REGISTRATIONS

	Pre-Set		Spinet		All Electronic Organs
(A#)	45-7856-043	(U)	65-8856-043	(U)	Flutes 8', 4', Strings 8'
(A#)	00-5543-100	(L)	3543-1000	(L)	Diapason 8'
Pedal:	5-3	Pedal:	3	Pedal:	16', Medium
Vibrato:	3	Vibrato:	Normal	Vibrato:	Full

Moderately

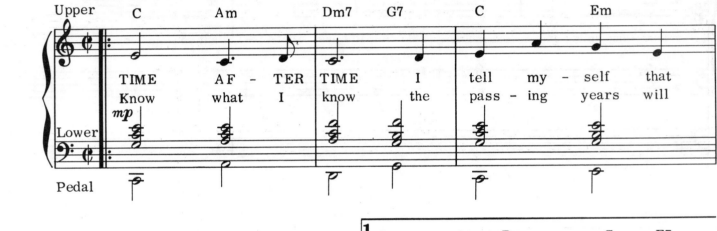

TIME AF - TER TIME I tell my - self that
Know what I know the pass - ing years will

I'm so luck - y to be lov - ing you, So
show you've kept my love so

luck - y to be the one you run to see in the

ZING! WENT THE STRINGS OF MY HEART

Words and Music by
JAMES F. HANLEY

SUGGESTED REGISTRATIONS

	Pre-Set		Spinet		All Electronic Organs
(A#)	40-8757-234	(U)	60-8757-234	(U)	Full Solo Combination (Strings and Reeds) with 16'
[A#]	00-6644-322	[L]	4644-3220	[L]	Great (No Reeds) 8'
Pedal:	5-3	Pedal:	3	Pedal:	Bourdon 16', 8'
Vibrato:	3	Vibrato:	Normal	Vibrato:	Medium

HOW LONG HAS THIS BEEN GOING ON?

Music and Lyrics by
GEORGE GERSHWIN and IRA GERSHWIN

SUGGESTED REGISTRATIONS

58

BLUES IN THE NIGHT
(My Mama Done Tol' Me)

Words by
JOHNNY MERCER

SUGGESTED REGISTRATIONS

Music by
HAROLD ARLEN

Pre-Set		Spinet		All Electronic Organs	
(A#)	00-7865-000	(U)	20-8865-000	(U)	Horn Diapason 8'
(A#)	00-5635-000	(L)	3635-0000		French Horn 8'
				(L)	Flute 8', Violina 8'
Pedal: 5-3		Pedal: 3		Pedal: Tibia 16'	
Vibrato: 3		Vibrato: Normal		Vibrato: Full	

IT HAD TO BE YOU

Words by
GUS KAHN

Music by
ISHAM JONES

SUGGESTED REGISTRATIONS

Pre-Set		Spinet		All Electronic Organs	
Ⓐ⚹	20-4625-000	Ⓤ	40-6625-000	Ⓤ	Strings 8', Clarinet 8'
[A⚹]	00-4423-220	[L]	2423-2200	[L]	Flute 4', Strings 4'
Pedal: 4-2		Pedal: 2		Pedal: Flute 8'	
Vibrato: 3		Vibrato: Normal		Vibrato: Full	

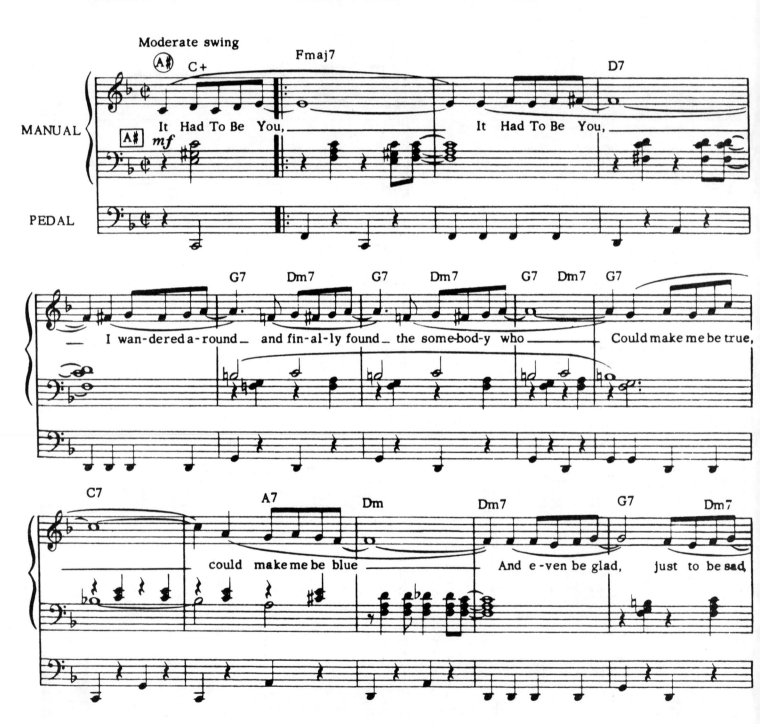

SOMETIMES I'M HAPPY

Words by
IRVING CAESAR

Music by
VINCENT YOUMANS

SUGGESTED REGISTRATIONS

Pre-Set		Spinet		All Electronic Organs	
Ⓐ♯	50-8746-224	Ⓤ	70-8746-224	Ⓤ	Flutes 8′, 4′
Ⓐ♯	00-4544-220	Ⓛ	2524-2200	Ⓛ	Diap., Gamba 8′, Flute 4′
Pedal:	5-3	Pedal:	3	Pedal:	16′, 8′, Medium
Vibrato:	3	Vibrato:	Normal	Vibrato:	Full

HALLELUJAH!

Words by
LEO ROBIN and CLIFFORD GREY

SUGGESTED REGISTRATIONS

Music by
VINCENT YOUMANS

Pre-Set	Spinet	All Electronic Organs
Ⓐ♯ 40-8757-234	Ⓤ 60-8757-234	Ⓤ Full Solo Combination (Strings and Reeds) with 16'
⬛A♯ 00-6644-322	Ⓛ 4644-3220	Ⓛ Great (No Reeds) 8'
Pedal: 5-3	Pedal: 3	Pedal: Bourdon 16', 8'
Vibrato: 3	Vibrato: Normal	Vibrato: Medium

ALL THIS AND HEAVEN TOO

Words by
EDDIE DeLANGE

Music by
JIMMY VAN HEUSEN

SUGGESTED REGISTRATIONS

Pre-Set	Spinet	All Electronic Organs
(A♯) 00-8476-000	(U) 20-8476-000	(U) Flutes 8', 4', Clarinet 8'
[A♯] 00-5432-200	[L] 3432-2000	[L] Melodia (Fr. Horn) 8'
Pedal: 4-3	Pedal: 3	Pedal: 16', Medium
Vibrato: 3	Vibrato: Normal	Vibrato: Full

Very slowly

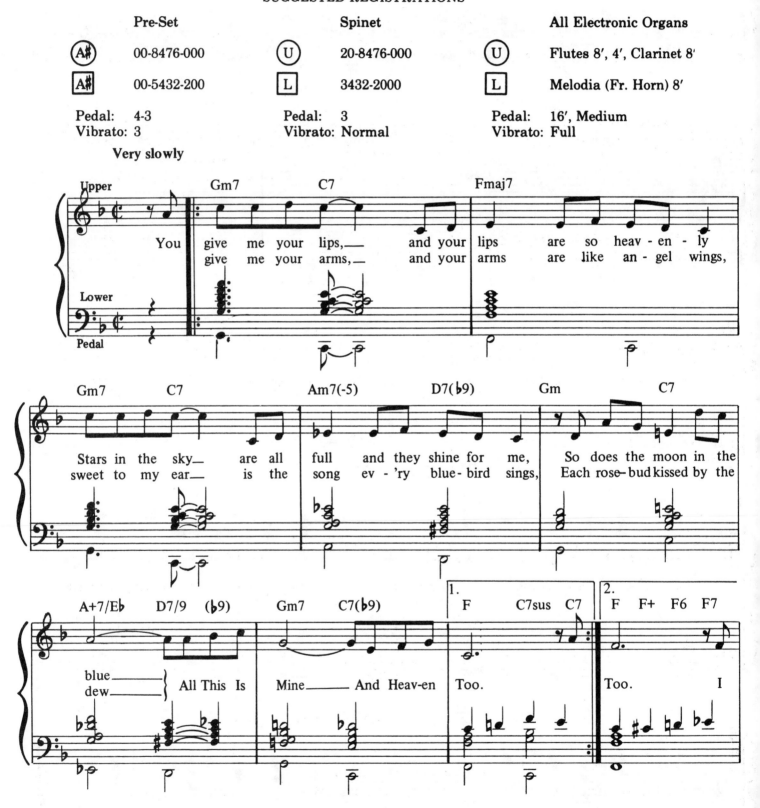

71

TOO MARVELOUS FOR WORDS

Words by
JOHNNY MERCER

SUGGESTED REGISTRATIONS

Music by
RICHARD A. WHITING

Pre-Set		Spinet		All Electronic Organs	
(A#)	45-7856-043	(U)	65-8856-043	(U)	Flutes 8', 4', Strings 8'
[A#]	00-5543-100	[L]	3543-1000	[L]	Diapason 8'
Pedal: 5-3		Pedal: 3		Pedal: 16', Medium	
Vibrato: 3		Vibrato: Normal		Vibrato: Full	

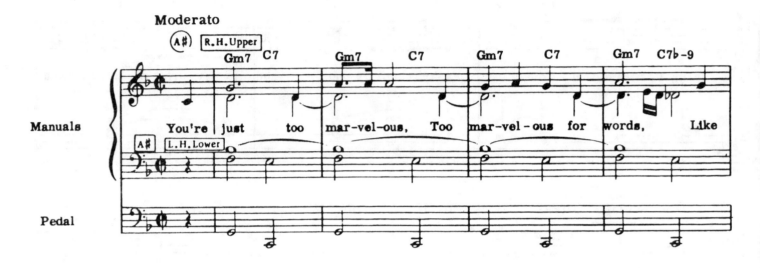

IN A SHANTY IN OLD SHANTY TOWN

Words by
JOE YOUNG

Music by
LITTLE JACK LITTLE and JOHN SIRAS

SUGGESTED REGISTRATIONS

	Pre-Set		Spinet		All Electronic Organs
(A#)	60-8800-760	(U)	80-8800-760	(U)	Flutes 16', 8', 4'
[A#]	00-6643-210	[L]	4643-2100	[L]	Geigen (Str.) Diapason 8'
Pedal: 5-4		Pedal: 4		Pedal: 16', 8'	
Vibrato: 3		Vibrato: Normal		Vibrato: Full	

It's on - ly a shan - ty in old Shan - ty Town___ The
roof is so slant - y it touch - es the ground; But my tum - bled down
shack, By an old rail - road track, Like a mil - lion-aire's man - sion, is

MY OWN TRUE LOVE

based on TARA THEME from the Motion Picture "GONE WITH THE WIND"

Words by
MACK DAVID

Music by
MAX STEINER

SUGGESTED REGISTRATIONS

Pre-Set		Spinet		All Electronic Organs	
(A#)	60-8800-760	(U)	80-8800-760	(U)	Flutes 16', 8', 4'
[A#]	00-6643-210	[L]	4643-2100	[L]	Geigen (Str.) Diapason 8'
Pedal:	5-4	Pedal:	4	Pedal:	16', 8'
Vibrato:	3	Vibrato:	Normal	Vibrato:	Full

APRIL IN PARIS

Words by
E.Y HARBURG

SUGGESTED REGISTRATIONS

Music by
VERNON DUKE

Pre-Set		Spinet		All Electronic Organs	
(A#)	30-5803-000	U	50-7803-000	U	Flutes 8', 4', Oboe 8'
[A#]	00-4423-000	L	2423-0000	L	String Diapason 8'
Pedal: 4-2		Pedal: 2		Pedal: 16', 8', Medium	
Vibrato: 3		Vibrato: Normal		Vibrato: Full	

THREE COINS IN THE FOUNTAIN

Words by
SAMMY CAHN

Music by
JULE STYNE

Pre-Set	SUGGESTED REGISTRATIONS	
	Spinet	All Electronic Organs

Pre-Set
Ⓐ♯ 70-8725-546
A♯ 00-6543-210
Pedal: 5-4
Vibrato: 2

Spinet
Ⓤ 70-8725-546
Ⓛ 6543-2100
Pedal: 5
Vibrato: Small

All Electronic Organs
Ⓤ String 16',8',4' Flute 8'
Ⓛ Diapason 8',String 8'
Pedal: 16',8'
Vibrato: Small

YOU GO TO MY HEAD

Words by
HAVEN GILLESPIE

Music by
J. FRED COOTS

SUGGESTED REGISTRATIONS

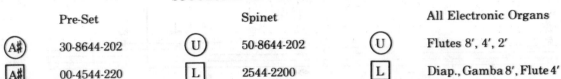

Pre-Set		Spinet		All Electronic Organs	
A#	30-8644-202	U	50-8644-202	U	Flutes 8', 4', 2'
A#	00-4544-220	L	2544-2200	L	Diap., Gamba 8', Flute 4'
Pedal: 5-3		Pedal: 3		Pedal: 16', 8'	
Vibrato: 3		Vibrato: Normal		Vibrato: Full	

Slow Ballad

You go to my head and you lin-ger like a haunt-ing re-frain

and I find you spin-ning 'round in my brain like the bub-bles in a

glass of cham-pagne. You go to my head

DANCING IN THE DARK

Words by
HOWARD DIETZ

Music by
ARTHUR SCHWARTZ

SUGGESTED REGISTRATIONS

Pre-Set		Spinet		All Electronic Organs	
(A#)	60-8800-760	(U)	80-8800-760	(U)	Flutes 16', 8', 4'
[A#]	00-6643-210	[L]	4643-2100	[L]	Geigen (Str.) Diapason 8'
Pedal: 5-4		Pedal: 4		Pedal: 16', 8'	
Vibrato: 3		Vibrato: Normal		Vibrato: Full	

86

THREE LITTLE WORDS

Words by
BERT KALMAR

Music by
HARRY RUBY

SUGGESTED REGISTRATIONS

Pre-Set		Spinet		All Electronic Organs	
(A#)	00-8476-000	(U)	20-8476-000	(U)	Flutes 8', 4', Clarinet 8'
[A#]	00-5432-200	[L]	3432-2000	[L]	Melodia (Fr. Horn) 8'
Pedal: 4-3		Pedal: 3		Pedal: 16', Medium	
Vibrato: 3		Vibrato: Normal		Vibrato: Full	

MY HEART STOOD STILL

From "A Connecticut Yankee"

Words by
LORENZ HART

Music by
RICHARD RODGERS

SUGGESTED REGISTRATIONS

Pre-Set		Spinet		All Electronic Organs	
(A♯)	50-8746-224	(U)	70-8746-224	(U)	Flutes 8', 4'
[A♯]	00-4544-220	[L]	2524-2200	[L]	Diap., Gamba 8', Flute 4'
Pedal: 5-3		Pedal: 3		Pedal: 16', 8', Medium	
Vibrato: 3		Vibrato: Normal		Vibrato: Full	

INDIAN SUMMER

Words by
AL DUBIN

Music by
VICTOR HERBERT

SUGGESTED REGISTRATIONS

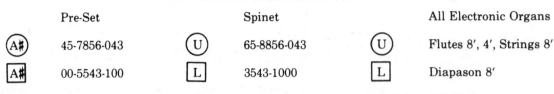

Pre-Set	Spinet	All Electronic Organs
(A#) 45-7856-043	(U) 65-8856-043	(U) Flutes 8', 4', Strings 8'
(A#) 00-5543-100	(L) 3543-1000	(L) Diapason 8'
Pedal: 5-3	Pedal: 3	Pedal: 16', Medium
Vibrato: 3	Vibrato: Normal	Vibrato: Full

YOUNG AT HEART

Words by
CAROLYN LEIGH

SUGGESTED REGISTRATIONS

Music by
JOHNNY RICHARDS

DON'T FENCE ME IN

SUGGESTED REGISTRATIONS

Words and Music by
COLE PORTER

LA VIE EN ROSE

Music by
LOUIGUY

Original French Lyrics by
EDITH PIAF
English Lyrics by
MACK DAVID

SUGGESTED REGISTRATIONS

Pre-Set	Spinet	All Electronic Organs
(A#) 30-5803-000	(U) 50-7803-000	(U) Flutes 8', 4', Oboe 8'
[A#] 00-4423-000	[L] 2423-0000	[L] String Diapason 8'
Pedal: 4-2	Pedal: 2	Pedal: 16', 8', Medium
Vibrato: 3	Vibrato: Normal	Vibrato: Full

102

LOVE FOR SALE

Words and Music by
COLE PORTER

SUGGESTED REGISTRATIONS

	Pre-Set		Spinet		All Electronic Organs
A#	50-8746-224	**U**	70-8746-224	**U**	Flutes 8', 4'
A#	00-4544-220	**L**	2524-2200	**L**	Diap., Gamba 8', Flute 4'
Pedal: 5-3		Pedal: 3		Pedal: 16', 8', Medium	
Vibrato: 3		Vibrato: Normal		Vibrato: Full	

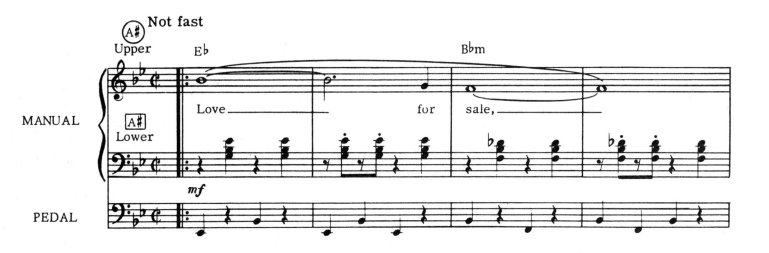

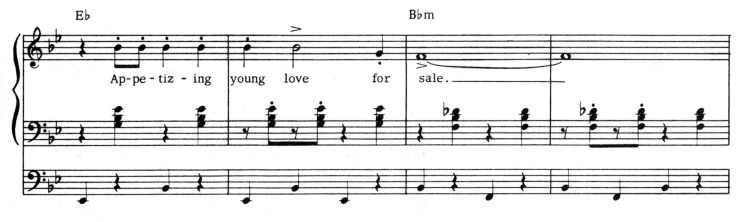

106

DO NOTHIN' TILL YOU HEAR FROM ME

Words by
BOB RUSSELL

SUGGESTED REGISTRATIONS

Music by
DUKE ELLINGTON

AVALON

Words by
AL JOLSON and B.G. DeSYLVA

Music by
VINCENT ROSE

SUGGESTED REGISTRATIONS

Pre-Set		Spinet		All Electronic Organs	
Ⓐ♯	50-6824-464	Ⓤ	70-8824-464	Ⓤ	Flutes 16', 4'
A♯	00-4544-220	L	2544-2200	L	Diap., Gamba 8', Flute 4'
Pedal: 5-3		Pedal: 3		Pedal: 16', 8'	
Vibrato: 3		Vibrato: Normal		Vibrato: Full	

A STRING OF PEARLS

Words by
EDDIE DeLANGE

SUGGESTED REGISTRATIONS

Music by
JERRY GRAY

I GOT RHYTHM

Music and Lyrics by
GEORGE GERSHWIN and IRA GERSHWIN

SUGGESTED REGISTRATIONS

	Pre-Set		Spinet		All Electronic Organs
(A#)	50-6824-464	(U)	70-8824-464	(U)	Flutes 16', 4'
[A#]	00-4544-220	[L]	2544-2200	[L]	Diap., Gamba 8', Flute 4'
Pedal: 5-3		Pedal: 3		Pedal: 16', 8'	
Vibrato: 3		Vibrato: Normal		Vibrato: Full	

YOU DO SOMETHING TO ME

Words and Music by
COLE PORTER

SUGGESTED REGISTRATIONS

Pre-Set		Spinet		All Electronic Organs
(A♯)	52-6070-542	(U)	72-8070-542	Strings 8′, Flutes 16′, 8′, 4′
[A♯]	00-4544-220	[L]	2544-2200	Diap., Gamba 8′, Flute 4′
Pedal: 4-3		Pedal: 3		Pedal: 16′, 8′
Vibrato: 3		Vibrato: Normal		Vibrato: Full

SOFTLY, AS IN A MORNING SUNRISE

Words by
OSCAR HAMMERSTEIN II

Music by
SIGMUND ROMBERG

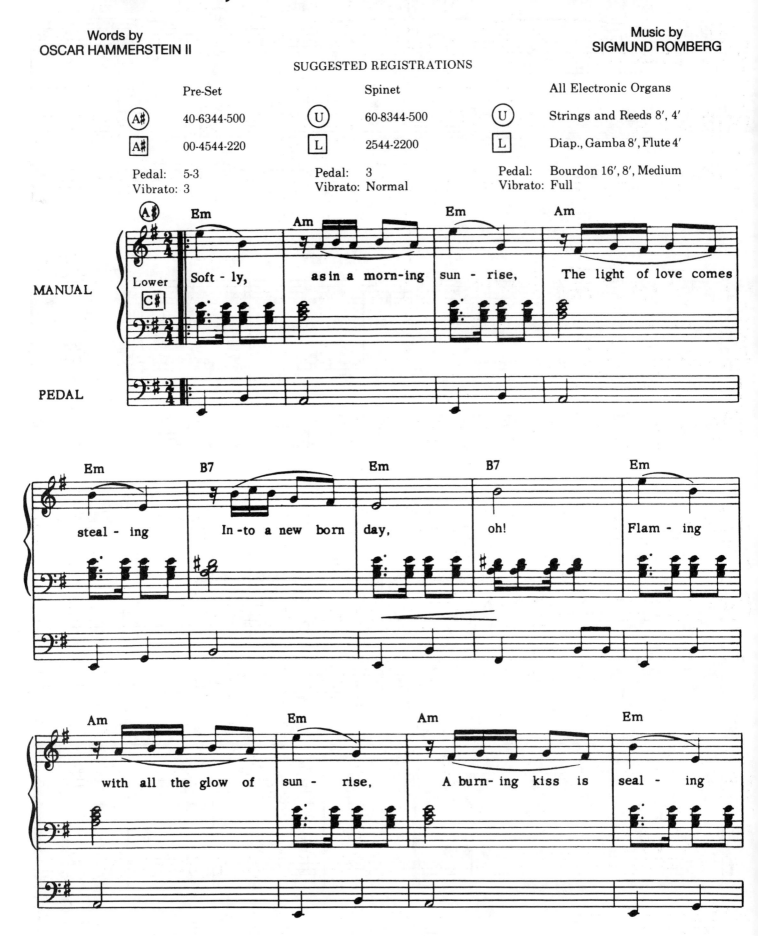

THE MAN I LOVE

Music and Lyrics by
GEORGE GERSHWIN and IRA GERSHWIN

SUGGESTED REGISTRATIONS

Pre-Set		Spinet		All Electronic Organs	
(A#)	50-6824-464	(U)	70-8824-464	(U)	Flutes 16', 4'
[A#]	00-4544-220	[L]	2544-2200	[L]	Diap., Gamba 8', Flute 4'
Pedal: 5-3		Pedal: 3		Pedal: 16', 8'	
Vibrato: 3		Vibrato: Normal		Vibrato: Full	

OH, LADY BE GOOD!

Music and Lyrics by
GEORGE GERSHWIN and IRA GERSHWIN

SUGGESTED REGISTRATIONS

	Pre-Set		Spinet		All Electronic Organs
(A♯)	50-6824-464	(U)	70-8824-464	(U)	Flutes 16′, 4′
[A♯]	00-4544-220	[L]	2544-2200	[L]	Diap., Gamba 8′, Flute 4′
Pedal:	5-3	Pedal:	3	Pedal:	16′, 8′
Vibrato:	3	Vibrato:	Normal	Vibrato:	Full

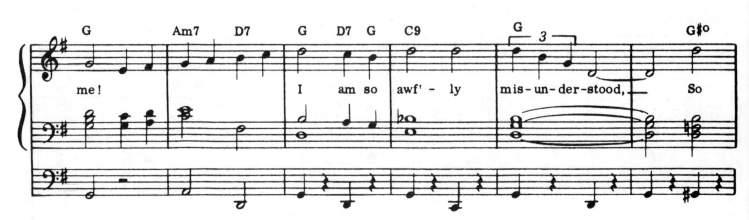

TILL WE MEET AGAIN

Words by
RAYMOND B. EGAN

Music by
RICHARD A . WHITING

SUGGESTED REGISTRATIONS

	Pre-Set		Spinet		All Electronic Organs
A♯	60-8800-760	U	80-8800-760	U	Flutes 16′, 8′, 4′
A♯	00-6643-210	L	4643-2100	L	Geigen (Str.) Diapason 8′

Pedal: 5-4
Vibrato: 3

Pedal: 4
Vibrato: Normal

Pedal: 16′, 8′
Vibrato: Full

BODY AND SOUL

Words by
**EDWARD HEYMAN,
ROBERT SOUR and FRANK EYTON**

Music by
JOHN GREEN

SUGGESTED REGISTRATIONS

Pre-Set		Spinet		All Electronic Organs	
A#	20-4625-000	U	40-6625-000	U	Strings 8′, Clarinet 8′
A#	00-4423-220	L	2423-2200	L	Flute 4′, Strings 4′
Pedal: 4-2		Pedal: 2		Pedal: Flute 8′	
Vibrato: 3		Vibrato: Normal		Vibrato: Full